IO099418

A Certain Slant of Light

Poems by

Barbara Novack

BLUE LIGHT PRESS ❖ 1ST WORLD PUBLISHING

1ST WORLD
PUBLISHING

SAN FRANCISCO ❖ FAIRFIELD ❖ DELHI

Finalist for the Blue Light Press 2017 Poetry Prize
A Certain Slant of Light
Copyright ©2018 by Barbara Novack

1ST WORLD LIBRARY
PO Box 2211
Fairfield, IA 52556
www.1stworldpublishing.com

BLUE LIGHT PRESS
www.bluelightpress.com
bluelightpress@aol.com

BOOK & COVER ART & DESIGN
Melanie Gendron
melaniegendron999@gmail.com

AUTHOR PHOTO
S. Rita J. Vanson, CIJ

FIRST EDITION

ISBN 978-1-4218-3810-6

To

Debby Usadi Nagler

who knows the seasons
and walks in light

There's a certain slant of light . . .
Where the meanings are . . .

— Emily Dickinson

Acknowledgments

These poems appeared in the same or similar form in the following publications:

Avocet, A Journal of Nature Poetry:
"January," "Jones Beach in Winter," "Sunset," "Sunday: 17^0," "March," "Seven Crows," "Affirmation," "December Sunday: What We Carry With Us"

The Weekly Avocet:
"The New Year," "Early April," "The Day After," "First Snow of the Season," "I Watch the Sunset Shift"

The Cape Rock:
"Prelude"

South Coast Poetry Journal:
"Pas de Deux"

Performance Poets Literary Review:
"Late January Blizzard: Aftermath"

Walt's Corner, The Long Islander:
"Evening at Jones Beach"

Creations Magazine:
"One Leaf"

About Poetry:
"Winter: 10^0"

Table of Contents

The New Year

The ball drops:
December 31 becomes January 1.
The new year emerges
from its gift box,
shaking itself free
of tissue paper and
giddy wrapping,
stretches, yawning sleep
from its morning eyes,
and climbs up on the
window ledge
ready to catch all the sunlight white
and prism it
to life.

January

Against a sun-pierced white sky
clouds lie like arctic snow:
winter ocean.

Jones Beach in Winter

pewter sky
  slate sea
    salt scent
whipped
  on whitecaps

Prelude

The animals in the park are going crazy:
the squirrels swarm in multitudes,
dashing across the grass and back,
skittering up heights,
leaping from pinnacle to pinnacle,
skittering down to madly dash and leap once more;
birds wheel, billow and swirl,
moving masses of connect the dots;
and gulls clack and chatter in nonstop rounds
of dive, soar, glide.

The season is askew,
April in January,
and in the park
sneakered strollers stride
with giddy energy.
No cloud-puff breaths winter laden,
but unseen breezes issuing from smiles.
The trees are naked, the grass sere,
but the sky is as blue as a summer pool.
The sunlight is at the wrong angle,
not harsh winter light
that slivers all hope of warmth,
but something golden, all buttery softness.

Tomorrow it will be winter again
and we will curl against the cold,
dreaming of the time
the animals go crazy.

Sunset

Flaming orange fire
shimmerglows
to glittering gemstones
purple iridescence:
sunset on
newfallen snow.

Winter: 10^0

Glistening ice sugar coats
brown winter leaves
shivering
in the January sun

pale yellow
weak tea in this world
that craves warmth
bundled in wool
hats, coats, scarves
gloves and mittens,
feet crunching in
fleece-lined boots.

Icicles shimmer
from roof edges
where gutters glimmer
glazed
as cotton candy snow
drifts
in wind-whipped swirls.

This is the season
for photographs
on warm sand beaches, bikini-clad,
for gem-toned umbrella-shaded drinks.
This is the season
for gazing out
breathing longing hazes
on frosted panes.

Pas de Deux

An icicle stabs the sunlight,
then slowly pools
on the pavement:
two perfect crimes.

Sunday: 17^0

After a week of cold, this
day after snow
white lightly coating the yard,
a frozen rivulet in the edging
between grass and
spring flowers, unplanted,
like the dream of a child,
unseeded.

Sun melted corner
stretches toward the center,
a hand of light and warmth
reaching.

Shadows contain the cold
frozen white waves
flowing up against
the neighbor's garage.

Roofs are coated.
Wires still.
There are no birds.

Late January Blizzard: Aftermath

I

Sky scrubbed clean
a clarion blue
chill sun skittering
off the pristine white.
The world is still
but for the brave shovels
huffing into hills
of sugar-spun winter.

II

The gray sky glowers over
muddy mounds of slush
splattering wheels and fenders
and knee-high boots.
The world is a morass
of soggy surfaces,
car exhaust tainted ooze
and grime.

III

Sun warms the lengthening days;
slush lakes, browned,
become birdbath puddles,
and somewhere beneath
a daisy waits
for spring.

March

Filigree of late winter branches
bud bulbs still a dream
tans and browns against the bleak gray sky
and a dark still silhouette:
a bird perched
deciding whether to fly.

Early April

So much snow this winter
salted and sanded
so we could make our way
along streets glinting with an icy sheen.
Now salt's crust stains the walks in waves of white
taking the measure of melting
and sand, shifting along streets and curbs,
swirls like the Sahara
in the warming sun.

Like a Robin in the Rain

black branches
moss leaves
slate sky
slick street

. . . scarlet azaleas

Seven Crows

Seven crows,
iridescent in the afternoon sunshine,
black shimmering peacock greens and blues,
peck at the April lawn
seeking seeds in
the springtime borning.

Seven crows,
yellow beaks gleaming,
peck the tender grass
seeking seeds.

From my kitchen window
I watch the seven,
shining black and yellow
amid the burgeoning green,
and I grab my pen
because I too have been
seeking seeds.

Affirmation

It comes overnight, the bursting forth;
it comes in a moment when the eyes close
in a blink:
from gnarled gray barren branches
casting stark street shadows
to leaf-fluffed avenues, all green rustling,
all dancing light.
It comes soft, the breeze borne sigh;
yes.

Summer Afternoon

I sit in my backyard
watching butterflies flit
from flower to flower
sunlight dancing
dappling wings like fluttering leaves;
feeling warmth glow through me
in this summer afternoon laze,
I sigh:
High on sunbeams, I
become the butterfly.

One Leaf

One leaf, tired of summer heat,
drifts down
on the lazy haze,
ending a season
in a moment.

Evening at Jones Beach

Evening at Jones Beach
on the end of summer-beginning of autumn
final-first day,
setting sun leaving opalescence in
the seasoned stillness aftermath:
gulls circle silently
stalwart swimmers sit
boardwalk strollers pause to ponder
transcendence
as the eternal waves
chase each other
to shore.

I Saw It Today

I saw it today
beyond the full-bodied trees muscling
light from the ground
like bouncers
keeping me behind the velvet rope of road,
keeping me from the lake beyond
where I know morning sunlight glints,
the morning sunlight that cheers me these traffic filled
workaday mornings.

I saw it today
the geese rising, swirling into their traveling V,
the first russet glittering on leaves.

We've been saying
this sudden September chill, this
leap to November
is unseasonal;
warmth will surely return before long.
And yet,
I saw it today:
Nature's knowing.

The Day After

Bare branches against
a pale pearl sky,
bark darkened by damp;
wet yellowed leaves slick the street.
It is December now,
the year's slide
to the finish.
Holidays of light await
as we stand at the gate of
the darkest season,
hands lingering above the latch,
hearts mourning the sudden loss
of autumn's abundance.

First Snow of the Season

Feathery flakes
sweep the surfaces
of evening shadows:
roofs and lawns, barren shrubs
and branches
hold the light,
painted white.

December Sunday: What We Carry With Us

Cut down
and blanketed by Saturday night's first snow
gray in the cloudy Sunday afternoon
cut down
spring and summer
that lasted into autumn
cut down
the roses, red and pink
the tall unnamed wispy purple and wide-petaled yellow
grown from random seeds
cut down
all the colors:
sheared stems peek
from monochromatic earth.

We will string Christmas lights today
cutting bleakness
at the root,
shearing starkness
at the stem.
And they will glisten on the snow
like flowers
and they will color the night
with their gem-like glow;
they will fill the dark with the ever-spark
of bloom and blossom: hope.

I Watch the Sunset Shift

I watch the sunset shift with the seasons
winter, southwest, to summer, west,
kitchen windows frame those season centers
as orange, pink, purple color the clouds
streaking across the sky.

I watch the sunset shift
with the seasons of my life
summer to winter
spring and fall between
the almost ages best remembered
as seedlings and ripenings
not the burgeoning forth or
the hunkering down
not the blazing length of days
or the chill short remainder
not the then, not the now
but the sweeter time
between.

About the Author

Barbara Novack is Writer-in-Residence and member of the English Department at Molloy College. She founded and hosts Poetry Events and Author Afternoons there and, off-campus, presents creative writing programs and workshops. Her recent books include the novel *J.W. Valentine*, nominated for a Pulitzer Prize and finalist for Pushcart Press Editor's Book Award, full-length poetry collection *Something Like Life*, and the chapbook *Do Houses Dream?*, finalist for the Blue Light Press Poetry Prize (2015). She is listed in the *Directory of American Poets and Fiction Writers* and *Who's Who of American Women*. Her website is www.barbaranovack.com.

www.ingramcontent.com/pod-product-compliance
Lightning Source LLC
Chambersburg PA
CBHW021917040426

42447CB00007B/908